Meteorologists

by Sandra J. Christian, M.Ed.

Consultant:
Joseph Moran, Ph.D.
Meteorologist, Education Program
American Meteorological Society

Bridgestone Books
an imprint of Capstone Press
Mankato, Minnesota

Bridgestone Books are published by Capstone Press
151 Good Counsel Drive, P.O. Box 669, Mankato, Minnesota 56002
http://www.capstone-press.com

Library of Congress Cataloging-in-Publication Data
Christian, Sandra J.
    Meteorologists/by Sandra J. Christian.
    p. cm.—(Community helpers)
    Includes bibliographical references and index.
    Summary: A simple introduction to the work meteorologists do, discussing where they
work, the tools that they use, and their importance to the community they serve.
    ISBN 0-7368-1130-3
    1. Meteorology—Juvenile literature. 2. Weather forecasting—Juvenile literature.
3. Meteorologists—Juvenile literature. [1. Meteorologists. 2. Meteorology. 3. Weather
forecasting. 4. Occupations.] I. Title. II. Community helpers (Mankato, Minn.)
QC863.5 .C48 2002
551.5—dc21   2001003330

Editorial Credits
Megan Schoeneberger, editor; Karen Risch, product planning editor; Linda Clavel, cover
    production designer and illustrator; Katy Kudela, photo researcher

Photo Credits
Capstone Press/Gregg Andersen, 4; Gary Sundermeyer, 12, 14, 20
Daniel E. Hodges, 8
DAVID R. FRAZIER Photolibrary, 6
International Stock/Peter Tenzer, 10
PhotoDisc, Inc., 16
Shaffer Photography/James L. Shaffer, 18
Tom and Therisa Stack/TOM STACK & ASSOCIATES, cover

**Bridgestone Books thanks KEYC-TV Mankato, Minnesota, for providing photo shoot
locations and props.**

1 2 3 4 5 6 07 06 05 04 03 02

Table of Contents

Meteorologists

Meteorologists study weather. They learn what happens in the atmosphere. They then forecast what kind of weather will happen next. They say if the weather will be hot or cold. They tell people if the sky will be clear or cloudy.

atmosphere
the mix of gases that surrounds Earth

What Meteorologists Do

Meteorologists study air pressure, wind, and clouds. They send weather balloons into the sky to learn about the atmosphere. Meteorologists measure rainfall and snowfall. They read weather maps. They watch for storms. They warn people about unsafe weather.

air pressure
the weight of air on a surface

7

Where Meteorologists Work

Meteorologists work indoors and outdoors. They forecast the weather for TV or radio stations. They may work at airports, weather stations, or on ships. Some meteorologists also teach at colleges.

college
a place where students study after high school

Types of Meteorologists

Media weathercasters forecast the weather on radio, on TV, and in newspapers. Some meteorologists work for airports or the government. Other meteorologists are teachers or research scientists.

research scientist
a meteorologist who does weather experiments

Tools Meteorologists Use

Meteorologists use many tools to study weather. They use maps, charts, and computers. They use barometers to measure air pressure. Radar shows where rain is falling and how strong storms are. Satellites circle Earth to take pictures of clouds and storm systems.

satellite
a spacecraft that circles Earth

What Meteorologists Wear

Meteorologists dress for the weather. They wear raincoats when it rains. They stay warm in coats, hats, and gloves in cold weather. They wear light clothing if the weather is hot. Meteorologists who work indoors often wear business clothing such as suits and dresses.

Meteorologists and School

Meteorologists must finish college. They study science and math. They learn how to use computers. Some meteorologists go to more school after college. They become professors or research scientists. Meteorologists never stop learning about weather.

science
the study of nature by testing, experimenting, and measuring

People Who Help Meteorologists

Many people help meteorologists.
Police officers and volunteers look for
signs of unsafe weather. Programmers
write computer programs that help
forecast the weather. Meteorologists
work together by sharing weather facts.

volunteer
someone who offers to
do a job without pay

19

How Meteorologists Help Others

Meteorologists help people make plans and stay safe. Weather forecasts help farmers know when to plant crops. Meteorologists also help pilots know when it is safe to fly.

Hands On: Make a Barometer

Barometers measure air pressure. High pressure usually means fair weather. Low pressure usually means stormy weather.

What You Need

Small, empty coffee can
Plastic wrap
Rubber band
Drinking straw
Clear tape
Index card
Pencil

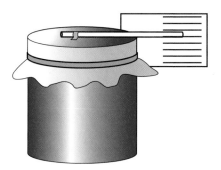

What You Do

1. Cover the top of the coffee can tightly with plastic wrap. Hold the plastic wrap in place with the rubber band.
2. Tape the straw onto the plastic wrap so that about one-third of it sticks out over the edge.
3. Tape the index card to the can behind the straw. Look at the picture for help.
4. With a pencil, mark where the straw rests on the index card.
5. Place your barometer away from direct light. Check it at the same time every day for at least one week. When air pressure is high, it pushes down on the plastic wrap. The straw goes up. When air pressure is low, the straw goes down.

Words to Know

air pressure (AIR PRESH-ur)—the weight of air on a surface

barometer (buh-ROM-uh-tur)—a tool that measures changes in air pressure; meteorologists use barometers to see how weather will change.

professor (pruh-FESS-ur)—a teacher with the highest teaching position at a college

radar (RAY-dar)—a weather tool that tells where and how much rain is falling

satellite (SAT-uh-lite)—a spacecraft that circles Earth; satellites take pictures of clouds and send messages to Earth.

warn (WORN)—to tell about a danger that might happen in the future

Read More

Breen, Mark. *The Kids' Book of Weather Forecasting: Build a Weather Station, "Read" the Sky, and Make Predictions.* Kids Can! Charlotte, Vermont: Williamson, 2000.

Farndon, John. *Weather.* Science Experiments. New York: Benchmark Books, 2001.

Hewitt, Sally. *Weather.* It's Science! New York: Children's Press, 2000.

Internet Sites

National Weather Service—Owlie Skywarn
http://www.crh.noaa.gov/mkx/owlie/owlie.htm
The Weather Dude
http://www.wxdude.com

Index